LONG ISLAND RAIL ROAD

by Frederick A. Kramer

Photography by John Krause

ISBN 911868-34-8

FRONT COVER: A scene from the days of steam, when Long Island ways were slower and the full impact of the Diesel Age was still to be felt.

INSIDE FRONT COVER: Steam locomotives crowd the engine tracks at Ronkonkoma. Keystone-faced these servants of the timetable make ready for commuter runs to Jamaica. Seven weekday trips began here at the end of the 1940's when the picture was taken. Just four years later, the number of originating trips was up to eight. Long Island's growth would soon turn into a population explosion.

Carstens

PUBLICATIONS, INC.

FREDON-SPRINGDALE ROAD FREDON TOWNSHIP
P O BOX 700, NEWTON N J 07860

INTRODUCTION

FOR NEW YORKERS, the jaunty and seemingly ambiguous phrase "out on the Island" makes a singular and well understood reference. Neither Staten nor Coney, not Liberty nor Ellis is *the* island. That term, by common consent, is reserved for Long Island, the great and historic front doorstep of America.

One hundred and eighteen miles long and from twelve to twenty-three miles wide, the land is shaped like a fish, its mouth hooked by Manhattan. It is incredibly varied and not like any other part of New York state. The Island's topographical potpourri blends plains and marshes, cliffs and bays, and reaches eastward in endless pines and sand dunes.

The east and west of it divide roughly into thirds. The western third, containing Brooklyn, Queens and Nassau County, was the Dutch part back in the 1600's. The eastern two-thirds is now Suffolk County, once the land of Indians and Englishmen.

Curiously, this one-third, two-thirds division roughly approximated the electrified and non-electrified portions of the Long Island Rail Road. The rambling eastern end was steam-only territory. Operations there were atypical, having little in common with the transit-like procession that emerged from the East River tunnels each rush hour.

But those multiple-unit electric cars making trip after trip, day after day dominate the Long Island's activities. Truly a road for modest distance commuting, the Long Island has been America's most efficient people hauler for decades. For the last generation, daily passenger count has hovered around a quarter of a million, one-fourth of all commuter service in the country.

But that busy scene is really the last chapter in a long and illustrious history. The beginnings go back to the age of sailing ships when the pace of commerce was slow and people, perforce, dealt directly with the natural forces that beset them. Since then, the sweep of events has worked its magic and left us with a most unusual railroad story.

Here was a transportation enterprise that tried several times to take advantage of the waters that surrounded its island isolation by opening combination land and sea routes. Here was a property of many firsts, some important enough to become the railroading standards of today. One such first occurred just as the development of the steam locomotive was approaching its zenith, for it was the Long Island Rail Road that bought the first diesel unit intended for rugged, over-the-road service.

Here is that story, briefly told in text and caption from the enjoyable vantage point of those who like to watch the trains. To them, long-haul passenger service held much greater fascination than the electric commuter scene. There was less matter-of-fact, grim determination and more emotion as steam locomotives came and went. The excitement in that greater distance, but subordinate part of Long Island's operations, is conveyed pictorially in this book.

Freight service, too, was incidental, for this was the only Class I railroad in the nation that generated less revenue from freight than from passengers — and by a wide margin. That uniqueness gives special meaning to the freight trains pictured here.

These photographs go back a generation to the decade following World War II. Their theme leaves aside the commonplace electric cars and focuses on the steam-to-diesel transition that occurred in the area east of Jamaica. Most are from the camera of John Krause, a lifetime resident of Long Island and a railroad photographer for most of his years. That happy combination of residence and leisurely pursuit now gives us a backward glance at *Long Island's Steam Finale.*

CONTENTS

A friendly greeting is added to the exhilaration of putting a fast and powerful locomotive through the paces on Captain George's Curve, west of Stony Brook.

By intention, Long Island Rail Road's main line stretches across the flats that extend mile after mile east of Ronkonkoma.

A BRIEF HISTORICAL OVERVIEW

THE WAR OF 1812 was over and America had won. Any lingering doubts about an independent destiny and a right to the high seas were forever dispelled. For a people who could still talk personally of their colonial days, those were buoyant and expansive times.

By 1825, New York City was foremost among the coastal ports, the first to have regularly scheduled transatlantic shipping. The Erie Canal had opened, making a "marriage of the waters" between the Hudson River and Lake Erie. In the process, New York became the Gateway to the West. With new trading patterns developing, the city needed stronger transportation links with the traditional ports of Philadelphia and Boston. Invention of the railroad suddenly presented a new way to strengthen those ties.

Connections with Philadelphia improved in 1831 when the Camden & Amboy Railroad crossed New Jersey, eliminating the circuitous sailing route around Cape May. But a railroad line with Boston was less easily accomplished. Connecticut's shoreline, pocked with bays and rivers and backed with rolling hills, could not be bridged or graded with any reasonable means at hand. An alternative approach was to travel the length of Long Island by rail, cross the Sound by steamboat, and finish the journey by railroad, eliminating the hazardous passage to Boston around Cape Cod.

The Long Island Rail Road, intended to span the island head-to-tail, Brooklyn-to-Greenport, was conceived as the New York land link in this alternative approach. Necessary action by the legislature was completed on April 24, 1834 and the Long Island Rail Road had its charter. The charter was to prove remarkable, for the railroad would be operated under its own name for the next 132 years.

Developing the charter privilege began the easy way. Instead of building eastward from Brooklyn, the new company leased the Brooklyn & Jamaica Railroad, a local venture that had started two years earlier. This step was provided for in the Long Island's charter and applied a technique that would quickly become a favorite in the new industry of railroading.

Then came the task of building, and that went a bit slower. New construction reached Hicksville in 1837 only to be halted when the Panic of 1837 dried up the flow of construction money. Recovery was slow, so that it was 1841 before the line got to Farmingdale, six miles farther. The final long strides to Greenport weren't a reality until 1844.

Ten long years in the making, the Long Island Rail Road had at last fulfilled its mission: the link had been forged that completed a through-route to Boston. From Brooklyn to Greenport involved a four hour train ride, then a two-hour steamship voyage to reach Stonington, Connecticut, and finally a run on the Norwich & Worchester Railroad brought passengers into Boston four hours later. The on-again, off-again three-part journey was a big improvement, faster and more certain than sailing ships. It was *the* way to go.

Completion was none too soon, however, for the prosperity of this through-route was short-lived. A railroad across Massachusetts from Boston to Fall River with a ship connection directly to Manhattan created a variation of the idea. The competition's route was somewhat slower but it avoided the transshipment at each end of Long Island.

Real — and insurmountable — trouble came in 1848 when an all-rail route was built from New York to Boston on the mainland. This happened less than two decades since it had been an "impossible" thing

to do. Changing times had wiped out the economic purpose of the Long Island Rail Road with an effect that was devastating.

In the receivership that followed, it became apparent that concentration upon becoming a through-route had resulted in a property that deliberately neglected, if not antagonized, local interests. They didn't forget, and that early disregard made the transition to a local carrier embarrassing and difficult.

Worse yet, the railroad had purposely selected a route down the middle of the island, an uninhabited area with no prospect whatever for immediate development. That desolate passage, that strategy for the utmost of speed, had become a monstrous liability.

Unfortunately, the Long Island's hardship came before the Industrial Revolution could support the era of railroad expansion. That would come later. Meanwhile, retrenchment was needed and it came in the

No. 50 dusts the snow on the way out of Smithtown. Heading east, next stop on this trip to Port Jefferson will be the historic station at St. James.

form of withdrawing the railroad's interest in the steamship service and operating at the subsistence level. The next two decades were quiet ones, ones of waiting.

Other railroads came into existence on Long Island starting in the 1850's, although competition didn't become serious until the 1860's. Generally speaking, the other roads had limited objectives intended to develop or connect local areas. But even in rudimentary form, those lines drained away traffic that had been moving crosswise on the island to reach the Long Island's rails.

The railroad needed continuing frugality. Coastal shipping kept great pressure on freight rates. As late as the Civil War, only two trains a day ran on the main line, just one of which went all the way to Greenport. Financially, it was simply impossible to build a branch wherever and whenever the enthusiasms of local people wished. By squeezing costs, postponing construction, and turning a deaf ear to the public, two

No. 39 could scarcely foresee that she was to survive the Age of Steam. Preserved by The Museum at Stony Brook, the engine has been given to the Steam Locomotive 39 Perservation Fund for restoration to operating status.

cumulative effects resulted: public attitude was galvanized against the Long Island Rail Road, and many people became receptive to the idea of approving and supporting other railroads.

About the best the Long Island could do to protect its interest was to build, or appear to be building, lines into areas that the competition was wooing. In spite of such maneuvers, two substantial rivals materialized — the Flushing & North Side Railroad on the one flank, the South Side Railroad on the other.

By the 1870's, things were completely out of hand. The Flushing & North Side had extended diagonally across the island and reached Babylon, ending right in the South Side's backyard. The Long Island, for its part, spitefully built its "White Line," a branch into Flushing that struck at the heart of the northern competitor. With such ruinous goings-on, resolution of this competitive situation could not be far off.

The bank panic of 1873 ended things for the South Side Railroad. It was bought up by the Flushing & North Side. The battle was down to two lines and hostility between the managements was intense, to say the least. When the Long Island's president Charlick died in 1875, the merger that was so badly needed became palatable to all concerned.

The merger was concluded in 1876. It was a key event in the Long Island Rail Road's history for it ended needless difficulty, broadened operations, and gave shape to something resembling today's network.

Since penny-pinching practices had left the older company in better financial position, the properties were combined such that the Long Island Rail Road was the dominant corporation. However, the Long Island's new president was Conrad Poppenhussen, the free-spending president of the Flushing & North Side Railroad.

One of the principal matters finally resolved was entry into Brooklyn. Twenty years earlier, 1850-style environmentalists had mounted a long and ultimately successful campaign to ban steam locomotives from the tracks on Atlantic Avenue.

Casting about, the Long Island sought a new western terminal. They selected the village of Hunter's Point at a spot in the East River swamps opposite 34th Street, Manhattan. Whereas the Brooklyn terminal was opposite the city of the founding days, the new Hunter's Point terminal aimed right uptown where things were developing.

That was good for the railroad but bad for Brooklyn. No attempt at horse cars or steam dummy engines on Atlantic Avenue could undo the commercial disaster caused by the railroad's absence. As the problem was political, not technical, it required time to heal — sixteen years in fact. Service was restored in 1877, but only as far as Atlantic & Flatbush Avenues.

All-night ferry service into Hunter's Point was started in 1871 and loaded freight cars were ferried starting in 1876. The biggest single item of freight was manure swept from the streets and stables of New York City, packed in tubs, and consigned to farmers all over Long Island.

Unfortunately, the new management failed to consolidate the house-that-Jack-built system that competition had fostered. They also failed to cut back on the unwarranted level of service and establish proper passenger and freight rates, now that destructive competition was over. In 1877, after little more than a year of failing to adapt to the new circumstances, the railroad again stumbled into receivership.

If ever a receivership was good for an enterprise, this was it. Needed changes were made, operating expenses covered, and a small investment in road and equipment was afforded. Improvements permitted a general speed increase to 30 miles per hour. No wonder the situation appealed to Austin Corbin, a visionary and great booster of Long Island.

Versatility was one of the strong points of this highly successful locomotive design. Designated class G-5, the 4-6-0 wheel arrangement engines could pull freight when required and make speed for long distance passenger runs when that's what was needed. They were best, all thirty-one of them, at the get-up-and-go, stop-again service called for on commuter runs. No. 30, seen here at Oyster Bay, was built by the Pennsylvania Railroad in 1928.

Rod Dirkes

After the Pennsylvania Railroad assumed control of the Long Island, it furnished the motive power. Like your friendly Ford dealer, the Pennsy offered both new and used models. New engines were built by the PRR in its Altoona shops specifically for the Long Island. Other locomotives were hand-me-downs, sold to the Long Island in the same way that the Pennsy sold obsolescent engines to short lines throughout the eastern states. In addition, the PRR leased motive power to the Long Island, not only on a short-term, as-needed basis, but also for extended periods. The leased engines were somewhat of a mixed bag, but PRR unstintingly included the successful Atlantic types and the outstanding K-4 class Pacifics, the very best they had.

[OPPOSITE, TOP:] No. 301 was an example of a second-hand locomotive. Baldwin-built in 1905, she served eleven years on the parent road as No. 2920, a member of class H-6.

[OPPOSITE, BOTTOM:] No. 4170 belonged to class E-3. She was leased for Long Island service prior to World War II and is seen near the old water tank at Oyster Bay.

[RIGHT:] No. 51, seen westbound out of a rural Hicksville, was a PRR engine, despite the fairly low road number. This was an E-6 class locomotive accelerating a commuter run, one of the things an E-6 did very well.

No. 112 and an unidentified Atlantic type race eastward at Huntingdon — not Huntington. The difference in spelling relates to the difference in terrain, for this is in the mountains of central Pennsylvania and the engines are returning light from major shop work at Altoona.

Projects interested Corbin. At the time, he was developing Manhattan Beach and eventually he would concentrate on the eastern end of the island. He took charge of the railroad on New Year's Day, 1881. During his sixteen-year term, Corbin would go on to complete the branch line extensions, modernize the property, and substantially increase the business.

But Corbin's greatest undertaking did not quite materialize. If the orginal go-to-Boston by way of Greenport plan was bold, his was far bolder. Corbin's proposed route was go-to-London by way of Montauk. He thought in terms of developing Montauk's Fort Pond Bay as a major seaport, thus saving a day on transatlantic passages. The beneficial effect of this plan upon the railroad's fortunes needs no comment.

Seaport arrangements were difficult to make. Corbin failed to gain approval for a government-built breakwater. Later, the Engineer Corps recommended against the overall plan because of fogs and turbulent waters. Nevertheless, Corbin pushed ahead, modifying his plan so as to make Montauk a duty-free port. It is generally thought that Corbin had personally lobbied well enough to gain sufficient support for Congressional approval.

The railroad extension to Montauk was completed in 1895 and construction work on the piers commenced. Just as matters reached the crucial stage, fate struck the telling blow: Austin Corbin was killed at the age of 68 in a runaway carriage accident. Without the able and aggressive Corbin to spearhead affairs, the grandiose plans for Montauk collapsed and they too died.

Crossing the waters that surround Manhattan was a key consideration in the Long Island Rail Road's next phase. Corbin had realized that the East River would have to be bridged or tunnelled for the Montauk seaport to have a major impact on travel. His initial intentions were to terminate somewhere near Grand Central, but as matters stood, up to 50,000 daily passengers still rode the ferries at 34th Street.

What influenced the situation was not an individual, but the Pennsylvania Railroad, that immense corporation which considered itself the standard by which other railroads ought to be measured. The Pennsy needed much better entry into New York City for both passengers and freight. The one and only way to expand its freight handling into the dock areas of Brooklyn was by means of the Long Island's holdings there.

In addition, a joint use of the proposed New York City passenger station would increase its traffic and importance. Perhaps these factors would thrust the surrounding area into a commercial importance as great as that of the Grand Central complex.

All things considered, the cost of acquiring the Long Island was acceptable and ownership passed to the Pennsylvania Railroad early in May, 1900. A new era had dawned.

The Pennsylvania invested heavily. The western portion of the Long Island was electrified between 1904 and 1906. In so doing, the road adopted all-steel passenger cars, a program that was continuously applied until, by 1927, the Long Island became the first railroad in the country to use steel cars exclusively.

Use of Penn Station by the Long Island started in September, 1910, two months before use by the Pennsy itself. Four tubes, drilled through the rock beneath Manhattan and under the bed of the East River, connected with the Long Island near the Hunter's Point terminal. These enormous capital outlays, far beyond the means of the Long Island as an independent line, were to have an important effect on the economic growth of the island itself.

As expected, the greatest increases in commuter ridership occurred on the Long Island Rail Road. Growth was steady. In the first thirty years of the twentieth century, island population tripled, while the number of Long Island riders increased tenfold — and still there were thousands of Dashing Dans as yet unborn. After all the heavy capitalization aimed at building the business, the Long Island Rail Road was finally able to pay dividends to the Pennsylvania Railroad in 1928. Dividends continued until 1933, but there were to be no more.

The end of the Depression did not end the road's financial problems. Neither did

One of the biggest post-World War II adjustments squarely facing the railroad industry and its suppliers was the question of steam or diesel power. Both railroad and traditional suppliers had vast resources of steam-oriented people and facilities. It made the decision far more than a simple economic determination.

[OPPOSITE, TOP LEFT:] Baldwin, the nation's leading steam locomotive supplier, had experimented early in diesel technology but a combination of factors worked against the company. One of the diesels they did produce was No. 450, a 1000-horsepower model of 1948. Because of superior truck design, 60 mph was set as top speed in passenger service, more than LIRR allowed any other switcher. [OPPOSITE, TOP RIGHT:] Fairbanks-Morse, on the other hand, approached the situation opposite hand: that of a diesel builder getting into the railroad locomotive business. The problem of market penetration to a level permitting economy of scale proved insurmountable. No. 1503 with an FM prefix and Fairbanks-Morse lettering was a demonstrator doing service near Stony Brook with a string of coaches in the old Tuscan red paint scheme inherited from the Pennsy. [OPPOSITE, BOTTOM:] American Locomotive Company's diesels were well received by the Long Island management. Their general purpose design was such that road switchers like No. 464 served well in commuter service. This view is at Glen Avenue on the Oyster Bay branch. [RIGHT:] The Fairbanks-Morse demonstration of 1949 did what it was supposed to do. It generated an order for eight more, as well as selling the demonstrator itself. No. 1507 was one of the new order delivered in 1951. Rated at 1600-horsepower, it had ample power to handle these four coaches over the Port Jefferson branch.

the end of World War II bring prosperity. If anything, things were worse. Regulatory intransigence held commutation fares at the same level they had been in 1918. Postwar inflation increased expenses, particularly taxes, and the expressway system was about to have millions of dollars poured into it.

The response by the Pennsylvania Railroad was to help the Long Island. They reduced rentals, postponed interest payments due them, and advanced funds for certain improvements. Unfortunately, the lack of effective public relations allowed the opposite impression to prevail. Many were convinced that the Pennsy was milking the Long Island.

It was no more Mr. Nice Guy after February 2, 1949. The Pennsylvania put the Long Island into the hands of the bankruptcy courts. Trustees were appointed and operations continued into 1950. In that year, two tragic accidents incurred claims of $10 million. The trustees resigned under pressure and it finally became obvious that a new approach was needed to address the Long Island's woes.

The result was legislation permitting the Long Island to end its bankruptcy and emerge as a railroad redevelopment corporation. With a maximum life of twelve years in this status, the Long Island was to have state and local tax concessions, a $60 million rehabilitation, and a $5.5 million loan from the Pennsy. The law was challenged by none other than the City of New York, but the state Supreme Court upheld its constitutionality.

As the end of the Long Island's statutory life as a redevelopment corporation grew close, it was apparent that it was all being done with mirrors. Back to private enterprise meant back to bankruptcy. There was nowhere to turn other than public ownership, the losses to be absorbed by taxpayers. Governor Rockefeller asked the legislature to establish the Metropolitan Commuter Transportation Authority and empower it to buy the Long Island Rail Road.

A price of $65 million was established for the sale of all the stock in the railroad. By assuming ownership in this way, the costly and time-consuming appraisal method was avoided. This was a generous sum indeed for a property that had no income-producing potential, yet far, far less than the Pennsylvania Railroad had invested. By excluding some of the Brooklyn freight facilities and extending certain tax relief, the Pennsy's pain was eased.

The time had come. What began on April 24, 1834 ended on January 20, 1966. After 131 years, 8 months, 28 days, the Long Island Rail Road was no more.

Nationwide, the lion's share of the diesel market was captured by General Motors' Electro-Motive Division. The Long Island, strangely, never bought any although they did exercise this GP-7 demonstrator in April of 1950.

Saturday's way freight heads home west of Stony Brook. The equipment roster reflects the overwhelming importance of passenger traffic over freight. Midway in PRR's ownership for example, LIRR owned 1400 passenger cars but only 2500 revenue freight cars, an astoundingly low ratio for a Class I railroad. Half the freight equipment was box cars, the type which predominates in this train.

Completion of the steam-to-diesel transition was celebrated, if that's the word, in an official and symbolic manner. White-faced No. 35, with one car, travelled west from the eastern reaches of the island. Meanwhile, No. 39, also with one car, started east from Jamaica. They met at Hicksville for ceremonies as diesels were brought up behind to couple up and take the cars back to the originating points. Oyster Bay steam service ended the following week and a fan trip the next weekend wound things up. Both engines have survived and it is remotely conceivable that this scene from October, 1955 could one day be re-enacted.

The men who worked for the railroad made the railroad work. [ABOVE:] The engineer of No. 21 scrutinizes the running gear. [ABOVE, RIGHT:] A trainman sets the switch at Oyster Bay for the station lead. [RIGHT:] Lenny Dick, ready to pilot a diesel run, went on to do his piloting on a commercial airline. [OPPOSITE:] It was the fireman's job to take on water, as is being done here at Ronkonkoma. [OPPOSITE, RIGHT:] Some brakemen catch a ride on the rear platform as it's pushed down through Port Jefferson's yard.

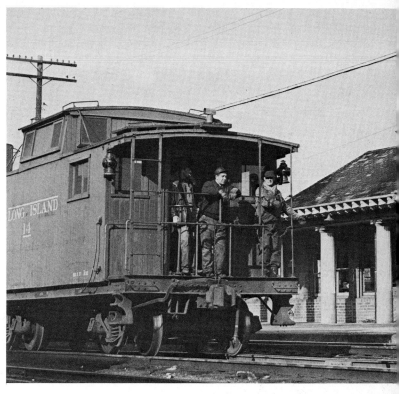

Rod Dirkes

JAMAICA

[OPPOSITE, TOP:] **For nearly twenty years, electric locomotives shuttled the steam coaches between Penn Station and Jamaica. During those years, the familiar "Change at Jamaica" was made by the engines, not the passengers. On a pre-World War II afternoon, Train No. 20,** *The Cannon Ball,* **arrived from the city under the old semaphore gantry. The multi-directional comings and goings were directed from Jay Tower, at center.**

[OPPOSITE, BOTTOM:] **No. 35, ready to leave with a special, poses two car lengths beyond the end of the platform.** [RIGHT:] **White-shirted towermen watch the special depart. In the midst of this welter of trackwork, soot, and sparks, there sits an island of grass — complete with plantings and, yes, a birdbath!**

The main line carries eastward out of Jamaica. Dense traffic makes this section excellent train-watching territory. [ABOVE:] A freight rambles by Denton Avenue, No. 314 in the lead. [ABOVE, RIGHT:] Local commuter runs were plentiful. No. 1238 hustles six cars toward Ronkonkoma in the days before air-conditioning. [LOWER, RIGHT:] Through trains bearing railway post office cars from Montauk roared past, this K-4 laying trails of smoke from the stack and steam from the whistle.

No. 32 accelerates westward out of Mineola on a right-of-way that was valuable for both rails and wires. The high pole line beyond the train carries power transmission circuits feeding Mineola substation, a third-rail supply point. The low pole line on this side carries railroad communications and signalling circuits by a combination of the open wire method from the turn-of-the-century and overhead cable that was a pre-World War II advance. Further developments in communication technology have made once-common railroad telegraph lines hopelessly obsolete and they have been dismantled as improvements could be afforded. The familiar blue-green glass insulators now grace the pages of collectors' catalogs.

MINEOLA

[OPPOSITE PAGE:] Beside a row of billboards for Broadway shows, No. 43 takes a curtain call at Mineola. The performance here is a morning commuter run and the script is all too familiar to the entire cast of characters. Except for the cantilevered signal mast which has been removed, present day changes are minor. Most surprising are the smoke smudges on the Mineola Boulevard overpass: they've grown bigger and darker in the twenty-five years since the clean diesels replaced the dirty steam locomotives.

[LEFT:] Heavy power used on main line trains, as well as on Port Jefferson locals such as this, paused for breath at Mineola.

[LEFT:] No. 1347 pulls up adjacent to the heating plant of the Nassau Hospital with an inbound train from Oyster Bay. She'll be in Jamaica in thirteen minutes, fifteen if there's to be a stop in New Hyde Park.

[OPPOSITE:] **Nassau Tower protects the junction where the Oyster Bay branch veers left. No. 24 comes in off the branch. Having slowed considerably for the sharp curve and grade crossings in the junction area, the engineer now widens the throttle for a bit of power to carry into the Mineola station area, a block away.**

[ABOVE:] **No. 38, midway in the junction curve, crosses Willis Avenue, momentarily delaying a motorist in his up-to-date Studebaker.**

[RIGHT:] **Outbound, No. 461 crosses Main Street. Built in 1948, this unit wasn't scrapped until 1976 and thus outlived the fifteen to twenty year life expected of early diesels.**

HICKSVILLE

End of track during construction in 1837 was named Hicksville, in honor of Valentine Hicks who was the Long Island Rail Road's second president. It was a 48 mile round trip from Brooklyn that required one cord of wood to fire the locomotive, plus another ⅝ of a cord to get up steam. Back in those canal age days, it cost a shipper $12 to ship a ton of freight to Hicksville. [OPPOSITE:] By September of 1947, many tons of freight were handled at Hicksville, the long train requiring men on the car roofs to pass hand signals to the engineer. No. 910 was a Pennsy class H-9 that had a round number plate characteristic of PRR freight engines. Judging from the size of the real estate shanty, you'd never guess that the business would amount to much.

[ABOVE:] Brakes applied, No. 42 rumbles in from Jamaica. Crates and barrels crowded the express office platform back when Hicksville was a small town.

[RIGHT:] Greenhouses and one-car trains consisting of a horse pullman, what else would you expect at Hicksville in 1947? No. 143, a Brooks design with conventional firebox, would end its career in less than eighteen months.

Hicksville was an important water stop with separate water plugs properly positioned for both east and westbound traffic. No. 113 works the Port Jefferson branch this day in May, 1949. [RIGHT:] A morning rush hour crowd awaits the arrival of No. 1508 with a train from Port Jefferson. In a few moments, the steam-powered freight will be heading out that branch on the adjacent track.

Cars and pedestrians, delayed by the passing freight, swarm across the tracks. The silhouetted figure next to the shanty is the crossing watchman bent over to crank up the gates. The tower operator gets added height from his platform as he hoops up a train order.

In the days of steam, the two-track main line crossed Broadway at grade and confronted Divide Tower, control point for Hicksville operations. The tower sat on the center ground of a wye formed by the Port Jefferson line branching left, the main line curving right toward Bethpage, and a connecting track on which equipment was turned. [ABOVE:] No. 35 drifts in off the Port Jefferson branch with a morning commuter train. Visible at the left corner of the tower is the boiler-top profile of No. 28, the "protect" engine sitting on the connecting track. Both the Long Island and the Pennsy used the term "protect" to designate fully operational equipment strategically stationed in case of breakdown.

[LEFT:] Rush hour over uneventfully, No. 28 leaves her protection position and returns light to Jamaica.

"No more pictures today, Johnny. It's our last day this week and we're goin' back as fast as she'll take us. You won't see us after we clear." Maybe. But it would be nice to have a shot of her, particularly if she were chasing the wind.

The roadbed was good and the track was clear; the fireman spared no coal and the engineer set no limits. Still, as they passed the platform at Pinelawn, there was a fellow who looked just like John, and with the same kind of a camera!

The cameraman climbed back into his sedan. You remember those Hudson Hornets at Daytona....

[RIGHT:] Steam power reappeared on Long Island in the 1960's in the form of a railfan trip using Black River & Western No. 60. The engine from New Jersey pulls the special past "B" Tower at Bethpage.

RONKONKOMA

Ronkonkoma's railroad station sits at the south end of town, a mile from Lake Ronkonkoma itself. As the town developed, the railroad dropped the *Lake* from the station name, although the depot carries the letterboards for both names. Ronkonkoma is an important turning point for passenger trains. There is a small yard located where the middle of the freight train is and a wye branches off to the left in back of the freight cars.

The Three Aces has pulled her train forward, just even with the west water plug and express house before passing under Ronkonkoma Avenue bridge.

On a different day, a group of paper boys helped the deliveryman sort things out before loading their station wagon. A station wagon of another vintage and purpose languishes nearby, its calls to duty becoming increasingly less frequent.

THE MAIN LINE'S EASTERN END

THE LONG ISLAND Rail Road of the early days had only one line, Brooklyn to Greenport. By the time of the post-Civil War expansion, the line's western terminal had been shifted from Brooklyn to Hunter's Point. It was to this backbone, or main line, that the branches would be joined.

Development of the main line proved difficult. The faded dream of providing a through-route to Boston was revived. The Long Island bought its own steamship, built a large stone pier for her at Greenport, and established the *Boston Express.* New locomotives and passenger cars designed for fast running were gotten to upgrade main line service.

Preliminary operation of the land-water route was started in the Fall of 1872. It lasted two months before being suspended

Milepost 82 crowds the Factory Avenue crossing, west of Mattituck. By the early 1950's, freight train L-63 performed her westbound chores on runs that left Greenport Tuesdays, Thursdays, and Saturdays.

because of rough waters. All the new equipment was brought to bear on the plan in the summer of 1873, but lack of patronage ended matters after just three months. It wasn't possible to turn back the clock.

The island's agricultural economy provided the bulk of the railroad's freight traffic. For moving farm produce to city markets, the Long Island tried the then novel method of carrying wagons on flatcars. Since the wagons of the 1880's were horse-drawn, stock cars were included on the train so farmers would have their teams on hand for city deliveries. Remarkably, the Long Island Rail Road had invented one of today's most important classes of rail transport — piggy-back shipping.

Increasing use of the main line's tracks made improvements imperative. The first double-tracking was from Hunter's Point to Jamaica, completed in 1874. This had been a four year project and not until the 1880's did steel rails completely replace the old iron ones. Just prior to World War I, the first of Long Island's major grade crossing elimination programs involved the raising of tracks and facilities in and near Jamaica.

At the other end of the island, the Greenport terminal was upgraded and enlarged in 1892. Shipside arrangements were im-

proved, new passenger and freight stations were built, and a four-stall roundhouse was erected. The roundhouse lasted only until 1921, although the adjacent turntable was retained long after steam power was discontinued. The brick freight house still stands, but modified so it can accommodate buses.

Not counting the short-lived *Boston Express,* the first name train appeared in 1885. This was *The Cyclone,* a Saturday only limited-stop run to Greenport. The famous *Cannon Ball* was established in 1891 as a Greenport train, only in later years to be synonymous with fast travel to the watering spots en route to Montauk.

Today's Wyandanch was selected as the place to terminate main line trains that did not make the long run to the east end. That was in 1884, but within five years, the point was moved fourteen miles farther to Ronkonkoma where short turns have ended since.

Mainline or not, much of the railroad's physical plant east of Ronkonkoma has suffered from attrition. Most of the way stations were torn down during the 1960's. Trucks move most of the freight and the railroad, a victim of the automotive age, itself provides most Greenport passenger service by connecting bus.

One-third of the nation's cauliflower came from Long Island. Steam power was on hand to bring a trainload out of Riverhead this day in 1951. Icing is required and waiting refrigerator cars are seen with their hatches raised. When potatos were shipped in these cars, they were not iced since adequate ventilation was all that was needed.

The loaders and icers had a schedule to meet. For both potato and cauliflower trains, the railroad dispatched an engine out of Greenport. It gathered any ready cars along the way and brought them to Riverhead. The engine would be available for switching as needed, but there was always a deadline by which the train would leave, all cars ready or not.

Beyond Riverhead, the main line curves northeast onto the finger of land that separates Long Island Sound from the Great and Little Peconic Bays. In early times, many trains terminated at Riverhead so that passenger service was infrequent on the eastern reaches of the island. As a result, freight trains accommodated passengers until 1884 when the practice was discontinued.

First station east of Riverhead was Aquebogue, a flag stop three miles distant. These 1950 views of No. 108 working there recall happier days. The hip-roofed station, at the right of the arriving train, was built in 1910. Not an agency station at the time of this photograph, the building was finally dismantled in 1967.

The mail crane seen in both photographs is now taken down, as is the diamond-shaped crossing buck. The cross street is Peconic Boulevard, now protected by automatic gates. No. 108 interrupted no traffic in the act of pulling a cut of cars from the potato house loading dock. Only the rearmost shed still stands, for even the silo is gone. The passing siding beside the main track and both leads into the loading area are removed. Nothing left, today's timetables, both public and private, make no mention of Aquebogue.

The afternoon sun pours its light on the spruce little station at Cutchogue. The suffix *ogue* appearing in many Long Island town names was the Indian word for fish.

The head brakeman escorts No. 108 down to the Young's Avenue crossing in Southold. By the time No. 1507 came by with the afternoon train, somebody must have needed something from Peterson & Van Duzer's storage shed because the door was folded open. A private siding permitted unloading directly into their shed. The keystoned W is a whistle post for the next crossing toward Greenport.

Southold, where settlers first set foot in 1640, has the oldest church society in the state of New York. Indeed, Founders Landing is a pleasant local park. Southold's depot is of board-and-batten construction and was notable for the comfortable surplus furniture that the agent put in one end of the public waiting room. SD on the signal mast designates the call letters going back to telegraphic days.

[LEFT:] Potato sacks airing on the fence on one side of her, No. 108 asphyxiates the potato bugs on the other.

[OPPOSITE PAGE:] In delightful silhouette, the Greenport freight crosses Mill Creek bridge at the neck of Hashamomuck Pond.

Greenport was the place that caused the Long Island Rail Road to be built. With a splendid harbor opening onto Gardiner's Bay, packet ships for the mainland connection to Boston were to put in alongside whalers and local fishing boats. Direct train service to Boston via a mainland route was ruinous to business and the importance of Greenport. The rails here are still called the main line, even though most service is by connecting bus and there is less of it than on the "branches."

"You want to do *what!* when you grow up?....Well sure, the Long Island's an all right railroad to work for."

GREENPORT

[BELOW:] **There's a pause in No. 108's switching moves as she sits beside the freight house. The fireman takes advantage of the moment for a breath of air, while a little boy and one of his heroes watch from the 4th Street crossing.**

Greenport yards in the February days of 1950. No. 108 pulls up to the coal pile. Refueling was done with an endless belt loader, but a boom crane fitted with a clamshell bucket was also available. Deferred maintenance on the water tank is obvious during its last period of usefulness, while the adjacent shed for the Way Department and the station buildings are in good repair.

OUT TO THE EASTERN TIP

THE LAST GREAT EXPANSION period of railroading in the eastern United States took place in the decade of the 1890's. Not until midway in that period did rails arrive at Montauk. This timing was in contrast to the line to Greenport, built on the north fork of Long Island at the very outset of America's railroad experience.

The first rails on the south fork led not to the wilderness that was Montauk, but to Sag Harbor, the other principal port at the eastern end of the island. That old whaling town was reached by branching from the main line at Manorville. Cutting straight for the shoreline at Eastport, the branch followed east through Bridgehampton and angled into Sag Harbor. The total distance was 36 miles.

Service started in 1870, just as the whaling trade reached full decline. But an event of March, 1873 had a far-reaching effect

In another thousand yards, the 106-mile run from Jamaica to Montauk will be over for the *Hampton Express.* One of four diesels in its series, No. 2403 was rated at 2400-horsepower, most powerful the Long Island was to own.

upon the area where the line touched the shore. A sea captain arrived with nine snow-white, plump ducks descended from the Imperial flocks of China. A new industry was born and Long Island ducklings were to become a prestigious addition to the railroad's traffic in foodstuffs.

At the metropolitan end of the island, the South Side Railroad had extended their rails as far east as Patchogue in 1868. After the island's railroads were consolidated in 1876, it became the Long Island's task to close the gap between Patchogue and Eastport. This was done in 1881, the same year that the grand plan for Montauk was conceived.

Rail service to narrow, sandy Montauk was justified only in the context of the great seaport that was to be built. When the dream collapsed, little actual purpose, but great potential existed.

One man who saw the potential was Carl G. Fisher. In 1912, he and his partner Collins had dredged some mangrove swamps to form a Florida bonanza they called Miami Beach. Fisher envisioned a repeat of his success by developing Montauk as a resort and recreational area. He built a seven-story office building as part of the master plan and moved ahead with the Montauk Manor Hotel. That three-story majesty was to rise on high ground overlooking Fort Pond Bay.

The Florida land boom collapsed on Fisher and the Depression buried all hope for his plan. But both office building and hotel survived the crash and they still stand, waiting for a Montauk that was not to be.

It was, instead, the one-word Hamptons that would attract the attention of most summer visitors. Starting in the late 1920's, the *Sunrise Special,* Long Island's most deluxe train, carried a through parlor car from Washington, D. C. and Pullman sleeper service was available directly from Pittsburgh, Pennsylvania.

Less auspicious passenger service was also operated, justified largely by the need to carry the mails. The line to Sag Harbor having become a spur in 1895, had shuttle service for four decades. By the end of the Depression, even the use of a gas car for the connection incurred losses that could be sustained no longer. The branch was abandoned in 1939.

An early victim of the Depression was the daily "Scoot" that served East Enders by a U-shaped route over both forks of the island between Amagansett and Greenport. Like that local train, Montauk's name trains also used the tracks connecting Manorville and Eastport. Those rails were abandoned in 1949 and since then the parlor cars from the main line have cut across the Central branch, reaching the south shore at Babylon.

Rod Dirkes

The costly and disruptive grade crossing elimination program was done in stages along the south shore. These pictures show the initial steps taken in Lynbrook in 1938, twenty-five years before the plan was completed as far as Babylon.

A temporary tower named Lynn was established at Lynbrook to control train movements during construction. Towerman Boerckel and signal maintainer Gayling step outside to escape the summer heat.

The temporary track is only at the tie-laying stage in this view at Lynbrook. The corner of the roof has been cut away to provide clearance.

Rod Dirkes

[BELOW:] **Construction is well along at Lynbrook. The concrete supports have cured enough for the steelworkers to prepare for placing the spans.**

[RIGHT:] **In a later year, the finished job at Lynbrook carries a sparsely patronized commuter run from Long Beach. The train slips in without the attention, let alone disruption, of passing motorists.**

Rod Dirkes

53

[LEFT:] The landmarks of Rockville Centre were unobstructed in grade crossing days. In 1950, temporary tracks were in place preparatory to erecting supporting structures and embankments.

[BELOW:] The grade separation program substantially eliminated local freight sidings, thus ending service being provided by DD-1 No. 340 seen switching at Rockville Centre at the close of World War II. While working the sidings with cuts of cars, the electric locomotives sometimes needed to stop in the middle of grade crossings. In such circumstances, idler cars specially equipped with third rail shoes energized the locomotives through jumper cables.

The finished product in full glory. No. 2007, wearing the second paint scheme, revs through Rockville Centre with a Montauk branch mail and accommodation train. The new high-level platform station is of the center-island type. St. Agnes church is on the left and, at the extreme right, work proceeds on the new Holiday Inn.

[LEFT:] **Steam and electric strike a split-second pose at Port Tower, 0.3 miles east of Freeport.**

[BELOW:] **A 1600-horsepower diesel brings a train off the Central branch which connects the main line at Bethpage's "B" Tower with the Montauk line at Babylon. This point is Belmont Junction and the rails will parallel the two electrified tracks for the remaining mile to Babylon station.**

The misty mood and variegated turbulence from the stack combine to form an artistic setting suitable for railroad calendars. No. 35, her nose well powdered with graphite, takes a Central Branch special under the signal bridge west of Babylon.

When electrification reached Babylon in 1925, the old frame station built in 1886 still served the town. During 1927, facilities were enlarged and modernized, an upgrading that lasted until July of 1962 when things were torn down to make way for grade separation. Like the structures, the equipment seen here is also long gone. Evidently, this is a Saturday picture, when the electric cars at left on track 2 and Train No. 6 on track 0 at the right were both scheduled to arrive at 9:25. The big diesel, having arrived via the Central branch, would soon be leaving for Montauk. The Patchogue "Scoot" will leave from track 1 at 10:05.

No. 2001 guides a railway mail car, coach, and parlor through Babylon under the care of the tower operator. In this particular paint scheme, the locomotive bore an LI within a circle as the insignia at both ends of the unit. Though the tower was built of brick, it was demolished as part of the $11 million improvement program that changed the face of Babylon. Seven grade crossings in town were eliminated, a result accomplished by elevating six miles of Montauk branch track and a half mile of track on the Central branch.

Long Island's only two Rail Diesel Cars perform their regular assignment, the shuttle between Babylon and Patchogue. This scene of the whole fleet is at the Robert Moses Causeway in Islip.

A quiet moment in Speonk yards. As the conclusion of the steam era approached, six trains a day terminated here, but by the late 1950's, the number had been reduced to three.

One of the world's finest steam locomotive designs, Pennsylvania Railroad's class K-4, disappeared from Long Island when diesel conversion began in earnest. Of all the engines leased to the Long Island, the Pennsy most wanted these champions back for service at their own last outposts of steam. [RIGHT:] No. 3655 pounds a swath of steel through the endless pines and [BELOW:] No. 5434 adds coal smoke to a steam plume like syrup to an ice cream sundae.

Rails end at Montauk station, five miles short of the eastern-most point of land where the lighthouse is. [LEFT, TOP and BOTTOM:] The crew takes advantage of every inch of the station stub track to clear the switch before backing down into the yards. It's a little past noon and this is the train that brought the final editions of New York City's morning newspapers.

[ABOVE:] Two grand dames of the passenger fleet repose in the yards. Open platform car 2038 is carded for *The Cannon Ball*, a train which, like the *South Shore Express*, ran both directions using the same name. [OPPOSITE PAGE:] Other trains returned to the city with a different name. Here, the *Hampton Express* returns as the *New York Express*. The view is from the slopes of the Hither Hills overlooking Fort Pond Bay. The majestic Montauk Manor dominates the skyline a mile and a half away.

TO THE WATERS AT OYSTER BAY

A THUMB OF LAND juts into Long Island Sound, Glen Cove to the west of it, Oyster Bay to the east. Typical of this part of the north shore, wooded highlands and rolling terrain connect the natural harbors on either side.

The presence of these harbors made coastal shipping not only possible, but far more comfortable and convenient than the stage coaches and freight wagons that inland folks had to depend on. Despite the uncertainties of ice and fog, water transport was just good enough to dampen the urgency of building the Oyster Bay branch. Financing, choice of route, differences of opinion — the usual railroad building difficulties — delayed the start and ultimately, the conclusion of construction.

The line was opened in segments. Service began in January, 1865 from Mineola to an empty field nearly three miles short of Glen Cove. This modest point was declared to be Glen Head, a rail head that particularly disturbed Glen Cove citizens who had

No. 25 rides the electric turntable at Oyster Bay. The engineer keeps a sharp eye on things, but matters are really under control of the hostler seen at the console just beyond the front coupler. No. 25, one of the low-tender engines used on shorter runs, was retired in November, 1951 and all steam service to Oyster Bay ended October 10, 1955.

helped finance the line to serve their town.

By May of 1867, rails did serve Glen Cove and four trains a day pulled into the station at Glen Street. In two more years, the asparagus community of Locust Valley was reached. Land holder opposition beyond that point was such that construction stopped there for twenty years.

The line had become the Locust Valley branch, terminating with a turntable and enginehouse facilities. Despite rail fares that were higher than those on the coastal steamers, the level of service rose to eight trains a day by 1877.

Locust Valley might have been the end of the line permanently had it not been for the threat of competition along the north shore in 1881. The Long Island Rail Road sponsored a flurry of activity that subsided as soon as the threat of a rival railroad passed. But the people of Oyster Bay, in turn, revived the action in 1886.

Definite commitment came in 1887 when certain lands were condemned and heavy construction was begun on the cuts and bridges needed to cross the thumb to reach Oyster Bay. The aspirations of thirty years were realized on June 24, 1889: steam trains finally reached the oyster-laden waters that had fed George Washington a century earlier.

No sooner was Oyster Bay reached than the old go-to-Boston idea surfaced again!

The plan was to ferry loaded passenger and freight cars across the Sound at Oyster Bay, reaching Boston through Danbury and Hartford over the tracks of the New York & New England Railroad.

As a rival of the New Haven, the New England line was seeking suitable entry into New York. By 1891, the docks had been built, steamers obtained, and joint service inaugurated. However, unsafe operations on the mainland, the adversities of crossing the Sound, and the general senselessness of such a route made the operation unattractive. It lost money consistently and folded after less than a year of operation. At last, the Long Island's involvement in travel to Boston was finally ended.

Today, operations on the Oyster Bay branch are controlled from Nassau Tower at Mineola. In earlier days, this tower was designated "MT," but Pennsylvania Railroad's standard operating procedures called for towers to be named.

Accordingly, the name Fair was selected, based upon the widespread fame of Mineola's Fair. It was an unfortunate choice, for as 1939 approached, it seemed infinitely better to have the tower at the forthcoming World's Fair carry the name. So in 1938, Mineola's tower became Nassau and, for safety reasons, the name Fair was dormant until it reappeared in Flushing Meadows on the Port Washington line.

Double track on the Oyster Bay branch ends at Locust Valley. When the dieselization period began, control and protection functions were performed by the Locust towerman. Today, the use of remote controls from Nassau has closed the tower. It still stands at the end of the inbound station platform, serving as an auxiliary post for Nassau County Police department's second precinct. Across Birch Hill Road, Vera's is now occupied by Maison Posh, Ltd., a subtle indicator of Locust Valley's standing among Nassau County communities.

What better way to try out the new Speed Graphic camera than to find a shiny-faced G-5 in a scenic setting between Locust Valley and Mill Neck. The date: December 26, 1948. The steamer had but two years of useful life left, considerably less than the new camera.

Two-thirds of the way through the S-curve at Mill Neck, No. 25 snakes her four coaches toward the city. Nominally the same as No. 41, above, there's a difference in pilots and tenders. Even the size of the numbers on the numberplates is different, the smaller-sized font normally used for casting four-digit numbers.

[BELOW:] **After the steam locomotives had made their last runs to Oyster Bay in 1955, a program of yard improvements was undertaken. The old wooden water tank was the principal landmark to be dismantled. Most noticeable additions are the pole-mounted floodlights in the lay-up yard.**

A neatly-attired trainman guides No. 1504 in a yard move while No. 461 sits at the station platform with her train. The round, white object in the foreground is a battery well used to power the track signalling circuits that start on this side of the lead switch.

No. 1694 strikes a classic pose at the watering facilities in Oyster Bay yard.

PICTURESQUE PORT JEFFERSON

AFTER THE LONG ISLAND Rail Road ceased to be the route to Boston, the need for branch lines was obvious, but a lack of money prevented an attack on this acute problem. By the outset of the Civil War, only one branch had been built and even that had been undertaken by others. The project was the Hicksville & Cold Spring Branch Railroad, operated under agreement by the Long Island.

In 1854, this branch was opened as far as Syosset where construction stopped, funds exhausted. Thirteen years later, it was the Long Island itself that resumed building, compelled to do so by the threat of a railroad along the north shore. The people in Huntington had, in fact, already spurned the Long Island and agreed to support the rival line. The Long Island proceeded to

Because the Long Island was in bankruptcy, court permission was needed to buy No. 2404 and her three sisters from Fairbanks-Morse. Delivery was in 1951, a year that saw the trustees strive for a separate non-PRR image. A string of coaches liberated from their past by a coat of gray paint follow the new locomotive under Hauppauge Road bridge, west of Smithtown.

buy out the competition and thus end the threat, but somehow the Long Island's rails missed Huntington village by a mile and a half.

The people of Northport, on the other hand, supported the Long Island and donated six miles of right-of-way in order that construction might continue on into their town. This was done and through service to Northport began in 1868. The Hicksville & Cold Spring link was subsequently bought by the Long Island, thereby giving it complete control over the Northport branch.

Farther east of Northport, railroad fever burned still brighter. Local citizens in that area went the people of Northport one better: they incorporated their own line, the Smithtown & Port Jefferson Railroad, raised most of the money for it, and leased it to the Long Island. As matters progressed rather agreeably, the eighteen mile extension to Port Jefferson was completed in 1873. The Long Island ran the extension and handled its affairs as if the property were its own. At the end of the twenty-year lease, a legal skirmish left the underliers with little choice but to sell their interest to the Long Island.

The extension to Port Jefferson joined the old Northport line about a mile and a half

from the end. By establishing this junction point, the Smithtown & Port Jefferson took advantage of more favorable terrain and thereby saved themselves some construction expense.

But unfortunately, they created an unfavorable operating situation for the Long Island. The spur was too short for its own shuttle, too long to back in and out of with Port Jefferson trains, and too important to ignore. The awkwardness of running some trains to Northport and others to Port Jefferson finally ended in 1899 when the spur became freight only. Passengers were accommodated at East Northport, served by a local trolley car.

Further extension of the Port Jefferson branch proved to be a mistake. For obscure and perhaps personal reasons, Long Island's president Corbin proceeded to build eleven miles beyond Port Jefferson to Wading River. Conceived in 1892 during the maneuvers to acquire the Port Jefferson extension, the extra part was finished in 1895. It was always a money loser and by 1939, the losses could continue no longer. What had been called the Wading River branch was cut back to Port Jefferson, right where it should have stayed in the first place.

Four miles north of Divide Tower at Hicksville, the Port Jefferson branch curves through Syosset. Then, heading east toward the dip in the land at Cold Spring Harbor, the drop steepens a mile before the station is reached. The climb out in either direction is less than 1-½ percent, but it is the more difficult for having Cold Spring Harbor's station stop at the low point. [ABOVE:] City-bound freight cars stretch back up the hill, pushing No. 106 past the station and a 1951 Packard that's enjoying its first summer. [RIGHT:] In less than a quarter mile, just above Eastgate Drive, No. 3740 works hard. It's right here that the railroad intersects the Nassau-Suffolk County line.

On Easter morning in 1950, No. 518 drew one of the few Sunday assignments on the Port Jefferson branch. The train is coming downhill on the Huntington side, a quarter of a mile to reach Cold Spring Harbor, 23 miles to reach Jamaica.

With the headlight cover open, No. 113 looks a bit matronly parading down the side track in Huntington. It's February of 1949, long before Huntington became the transition point between diesel and electrified territory.

No. 109 lays a little smoke cover in the woods that span the middle third of Northport's freight-only spur.

Northport's passenger station is now in East Northport. No. 113 has gotten her twenty-odd cars onto the side track to await the passage of a New York-bound passenger train. No. 113 was a member of class H-10, a group of nineteen 2-8-0 Consolidations that came from various builders between 1913 and 1916. All were ex-PRR and arrived on Long Island between 1928 and 1930. This picture was taken in the time frame midway between the end of World War II when stokers were finally installed and the end of steam in 1955.

[OPPOSITE, ABOVE LEFT:] **Although the Long Island could be justifiably proud of its new station building at Kings Park, the principal railroad attraction was the 1.3 mile spur to the grounds of the Kings Park State Hospital and the special passenger service provided there. Sundays only, a morning train brought visitors to the institution, a full ten minutes being scheduled for the cautious run over the spur. The train would back out, and then the engine with one car for the crew would proceed to Port Jefferson to be turned and serviced. After the crew had lunch, the train would return to the hospital.** [OPPOSITE, BELOW LEFT:] **With no less than a K-4 on the point, the return jaunt to pick up the rest of the train crosses the trestle west of Stony Brook.** [OPPOSITE, RIGHT:] **Principal commodity handled was coal for the hospital's heating plant.** [ABOVE:] **No. 107 works a string of hoppers in front of the administration building and** [RIGHT:] **No. 106, emerging from the spur, crosses Route 25A.**

It's a little past noon, one mild February day in 1953 and the place is Smithtown. [LEFT:] As No. 107 takes the side track, the rear brakeman swings off the caboose step to reset the switch for the main track. [BELOW:] That done, the seven-car peddler freight pulls up toward the station. [OPPOSITE:] Finally, in classic conjunction of the steam and diesel ages, a youthful Fairbanks-Morse breezily overtakes the veteran workhorse. Engineer's oilcan seemingly at attention and long skirts on mother and daughter add memorable ingredients to this bygone moment.

[LEFT:] **Trains from New York entered Smithtown by a viaduct that carried them over the Jericho Turnpike, an adjacent point of bottomland, and the Nissequogue River. This is bridge P46.31 and speed is restricted to 40 mph. Snow-splattered No. 1507 arrives under ominous skies.**

[OPPOSITE, TOP:] **No. 107 crosses the last girder span on her way west. Underneath, four empty lanes of the turnpike curve to the right on their way into town. At the foot of the hill, to the left of where the car is coming out onto the highway, stands the statue of a bull, symbolic of the event that determined the town's size. It happened that, in colonial days, Richard Smith tamed a bull for riding purposes. By agreement with the Indians, Smith's lands were to be as much as he could ride his bull around in one day's time. Judging from the overall size of town, "Bull" Smith put in a long day.**

[OPPOSITE, BOTTOM:] **Farther west, beyond Kings Park, No. 113 takes freight train L-57 across bridge P41.64, a five-span deck girder trestle. The cross-braced structural members, sturdy as they are, somehow leave the impression that it was done with a giant Erector set.**

Trains are particularly welcome friends in bad weather. No. 32 wears the face of reliability as she parts the snowflakes back in 1950. The platform has been shoveled, but there's no need to shovel out a path to the water pump in the side yard. This station building, one of the old originals, has been sheltering commuters from the elements since 1873.

[ABOVE:] **No. 107 comes by, singing yesterday's song. Louis Armstrong sang too in those days and his repertoire included** *St. James Infirmary,* **but this wasn't the place he sang about. Oddly enough, however, Stony Brook's station was indeed the place that Slim Gaillard wrote and sang about in his 1948 hit** *Down by the Station.* **Ten years earlier, Slim had won his popularity with his incomparable** *Flat Foot Floogie.*

[RIGHT:] **Flowerfield station was a signal stop a mile and a quarter east of St. James. By the time No. 38 steamed by in the early 1950's, the place had passed from station to residence and was only a few years away from demolition.**

Stony Brook in sun and rain, in diesel and in steam, with clear boards and with red boards, on main track and on side track. The solid rubber-tired express wagon didn't seem to change.

Peddling freight out in the countryside isn't so much profitable as it is necessary. [OPPOSITE:] **No. 111** backs into Bruno J. Beck's siding under the guidance of the brakeman visible just over the shed roof. This was 1953 and the days are numbered for outside-braced wooden box cars. [RIGHT:] **No. 107** crosses over Depot Road in Setauket. [BELOW:] Minutes earlier she had delivered a hopper opposite Setauket's station, a building that was torn down in 1960.

Fluted columns mark Port Jefferson's station. This became the terminal of the branch after the tracks were cut back from Wading River in 1939. Fifteen years later, No. 50 waited somewhat impatiently to get underway. [BELOW:] No. 21 is underway, the single coach signifying the Kings Park Hospital trip.

Port Jefferson's railroad facilities are 200 feet higher and over a mile away from the famous old port that built whalers, China Clippers, and dispatched the very last ship to make the rum, molasses, and slave trade triangle. [ABOVE:] No. 5455 and a compatriot steam up and [BELOW:] No. 107 backs down to pick up caboose 14.

An odd moment in Port Jefferson yard finds steam locomotives sprawled around as if it were never going to end. The G-5's, Nos. 48, 34, and 31, were all retired in November, 1951 and the K-4, No. 3740, had gone back to the Pennsy by then. On a G-5, the headlight was platform-mounted on the smoke box, and its turbo-generator positioned up in back. Many K-4's were altered so that arrangements were reversed, but the maintenance virtues of doing so exacted a terrible price in esthetics. [ABOVE:] Perhaps No. 113 is expressing an opinion about diesels in all that smoky calligraphy. [BELOW:] Nos. 28 and 35 are seen here in portraiture from the rear three-quarter angle.

Rod Dirkes

ALSO ON THE ROSTER

By the 1950's when diesels became the economically feasible motive power, the Long Island already had a quarter of a century's experience with them. [LEFT:] No. 401 was, in 1926, the first road unit in the country. ALCO, GE, and Ingersoll-Rand collaborated in building it for the Long Island. [LOWER LEFT:] Second No. 402 came from the same builders in 1928, replacing a gas-electric from J. G. Brill Co. that proved unsatisfactory. [BELOW:] For switching service, a pair of four-wheeled units was tried. This is the B-half of No. 403, a Baldwin-Westinghouse contribution of 1927.

Rod Dirkes

Rod Dirkes

Electricity was another approach taken in areas such as Bay Ridge to eliminate the smoke nuisance. [LEFT:] Nos. 336 and 327 are seen working as a pair, although they could work individually. Either way, these 1926 designs sounded like a rolling short circuit. [BELOW:] Pin-striped and just out of the shop, electric No. 348 waits to be towed back to third rail territory. Built in 1910 for PRR tunnel service into Penn Station, class DD-1 units were sold to the Long Island to do the same kind of Penn Station duty, only eastbound to Jamaica.

Rod Dirkes

Rod Dirkes

93

Rod Dirkes

The roundhouse hostler at Morris Park is in the process of bringing a beautifully groomed No. 34 out to the ready track. In the late 1930's, Long Island locomotives still carried round numberplates. The change to keystones came in 1942.

Rod Dirkes

Rod Dirkes

ALCO's Schenectady Works built this husky eight-wheel switcher in 1916. Designated as class C-51, there were eighteen in the group by the time the last one was delivered in 1924. Here, No. 254 sits at Morris Park's old wooden coal tipple prior to World War II.

Time out in 1937 to display the road-rail vehicle, a concept that periodically gets newspaper coverage as new and exciting. This old Chevrolet bore road number 1223, and had a ton and a half carrying capacity. The men's posture and expression suggest a justifiable pride in their machine.

Locomotive Rosters

Diesel locomotives   All-time to 1977

Numbers	Builder	Model	Built	Notes
100-107	EMD	SW1001	1977	
150-172	EMD	MP15AC	1977	
200-221	Alco	C420	1963-64	Lease expired, all off property by 1976
222-229	Alco	C420	1968	Equipped with Hi-Ad trucks
250-277	EMD	GP38-2	1976-77	No.252 in Bicentennial colors
398-399	GE	25-ton	1958	Shop locos
400	GE	44-ton	1950	To BR&W, 1963
401	Alco-GE	Boxcab	1925	Scrapped 1951
402	Alco-GE	Boxcab	1928	Scrapped 1953
403A-403B	BLW	Boxcab	1927	"Mike & Ike", 300 h.p. each, semipermanently coupled, retired circa 1944
403 (2nd)	BLW	VO-660	1945	Sold to Boston Metals, 1963
404-408	Alco	S1	1946	All sold by 1977
409-412	BLW	DS44-660	1948	All sold by 1964
413-421	Alco	S1	1949	Four pending disposition 1977
439-445	Alco	S2	1948-49	Acquired from D&H, 1963-64
446-449	Alco	S2	1949	Most S2's pending disposition 1977
461-469	Alco	RS2	1949-50	All retired by 1977
600-610	Alco (GE)	FA2 (cab)	1951-56	Rebuilt as power cab cars, see accompanying roster
611-618	Alco (GE)	FA1 (cab)	1947-48	Rebuilt as power cab cars, see accompanying roster
1501-1502	FM	H16-44	1951	Traded to Alco 1964
1503	FM	H15-44	1950	Ex-FM demo 1500, to Alco 1964
1504-1509	FM	H16-44	1951	Traded to Alco 1964
1519-1520	Alco	RS2	1955	Retired by 1977
2001-2008	FM	CPA20-5	1950	Traded to Alco 1964
2401-2404	FM	CPA24-5	1951	Traded to Alco 1964

Compiled December 1977 by Jim Boyd from data in *Extra 2200 South*, and *Steel Rails to the Sunrise* by Ron Ziel and George Foster.

Steam locomotives   1940 to end of steam

Number	Class	Type	Builder	Built	Notes
20-50	G-5s	4-6-0	PRR	1924-29	35 and 39 preserved
101-119	H-10s	2-8-0	Various	1913-16	
141-146	G53sd	4-6-0	Brooks	1917	
251-269	C-51sa	0-8-0	Alco	1916-1924	
300-314	H-6sb	2-8-0	BLW/PRR	1905-07	

Various PRR locomotives were leased to LIRR in substantial numbers for varying lengths of time. Classes since 1940 include G-5s 4-6-0's, various classes (mostly H-9) 2-8-0's, K-4s 4-6-2's and L-1s 2-8-2's as well as some switch engines.

Electric locomotives

Number	Class	Type	Built
324-337	B-3	0-6-0	Juniata, 1926
338-360	DD-1	4-4-0+0-4-4	Juniata, 1926

Alco FA cab-cars

LIRR	FORMER	TYPE
600	NYC 1102, PC 1302	FA2
601	L&N 317	FA2
602	L&N 309	FA2
603	L&N 315	FA2
604	L&N 314	FA2
605	L&N 310	FA2
606	L&N 321	FA2
607	WM 303	FA2
608	WM 304	FA2
609	WM 301	FA2
610	WM 302	FA2
611	SP&S 857, BN 4102	FA1
612	SP&S 856, BN 4100	FA1
613	SP&S 866, BN 4120	FA1
614	SP&S 858, BN 4104	FA1
615	SP&S 864, BN 4116	FA1
616	SP&S 860, BN 4108	FA1
617	NH 0428, PC 1333	FA1
618	NH 0401, PC 1330	FA1

In 1972-73, the Long Island acquired 19 control-cab/power-cars that were converted at the General Electric Apparatus Shop in North Bergen, N.J., from FA1 and FA2 locomotives from the L&N, WM, BN and PC. The units retain their Alco prime movers to supply power for train heating, air conditioning and lighting, but have no traction motors or dynamic brakes. The engines run at a constant speed to supply electrical power. The brakes and throttle controls in the cabs are connected via multiple-unit lines to the conventional locomotive at the opposite end of the push-pull consist.

Between 1972 and 1977 LIRR leased various GP7's and GP9's from Bangor & Aroostook and Precision National Corp.

INSIDE BACK COVER:

Fashionable and perhaps a bit bold, what with those yardstick-high numbers on the prow, No. 2008 was a Fairbanks-Morse C-liner bought in 1950. Last in a series of eight, the unit churned out 2000 horsepower. This was the first paint scheme to be applied to these road engines. In addition to the supersized numbers that proclaimed the engine's every arrival, the paint job was set off with a logo symbolizing service to the four corners of Long Island.